22 @ 22

Poems of Young Love

by

Tom Typinski

DEDICATION

To Debi,
Who let Love Reign O'er Me
Forever

POEMS OF YOUNG LOVE

TOM TYPINSKI

THE FABRIC OF OUR LIVES

One thread balances
the weight of our experience.
At times we hold it,
at others, we hang from it.

It mends our hurts
embroiders our success,
ties futures through birth,
pulls present through past.

When cold, it warms us.
When lonely, it comforts.
When all is lost, it finds us.
When forgotten, it reminds.

It's all we need ask
when feeling in lack.
It's all we began with,
when this "WE" began.

It's one thread of love
binding heart to heart;
one thread to fashion
the fabric of our lives.

(Anniversary Poem 1998)

LAST CALL

In the last, final minutes
before sleep overtakes me
when the silence is surrounding,
the night and the pulsing of my temples
a fading murmur;

As the last of day's thoughts
break and dissipate into disjointed fragments
mutating soon to dreams;
where the real meets the possible and
the past meets present and
finally the hum of machines and
the messages of tomorrow's to –do's and
today's should-have-beens go to dissolution;
when all plans and ideas, goals, dreams, and desires
finally subsume

leaving me only with your scent
and the sound of your breath
and the heat of your legs
I come back to where
I left with
one last thought -
You.

BIG DIPPER

If the Big Dipper were a spoon
I would fill it with my love
And ladle it on you

If my heart were the moon
I could hang it up above
to always shine, full view

If the Great Galactic Bear could croon
He would sing like a dove
Of how much I'm true

If these words could fill a balloon
I would float with you, My Love
for as long as the sky is blue.

TREEHOUSE

Let's be in a tree.
Just us,
you and me.
Helping the breeze out,
by shaking the leaves.
We'll scheme up some dreams
and in them, believe,
There in the deep dark,
deep
dark green.

With sunshine our window
and crickets in stereo
it's there that our love shows
a fantasized scene.
The sound of deep feelings
a murmur of screams
we've brought on a storm
without bringing rain;
lying behind branches
breathless
motionless
serene.

LUST IS A TERRIBLE THING TO WASTE

I remember dripping liquid
on your back
cool warmth
overpowered the bumps;
defeated, you lay relaxed
as my hands swept from
pelvic bone to scapula then back
down your spine,
thumbs centered and in seconds
the equation of mind meets physical let
you be mine;
a puddle of contentment.

There's a chip with the memories
of you and me
hidden deep within the network
We have only 55 zillion
I can conjure only 4
First Son
Second Son
Third Son
and last time
we made love
Lust is a terrible thing to waste.

LOVE

Just what are you
another 4 letter word

Are you this feeling that's in my heart
that calls to the one I've chosen
Are you her
Are you the thing
that motivates me
to do the things
I do
Is it you
that makes me blue
And happy

How do I get more
and what does it cost
And what good did it do me
if I felt it'd been lost

Love
Why are you such a mystery
and so selfish
Why can't everyone have you
Or give you
Or live without you

Just what is the prize once you're found
Is it simply the way you sound
and the way you feel
and the way you steal
Love?

II

A mist of less importance masks reluctance lost in the drizzle that
rain brings on.

Smashing bugs on the pages of self worth, while those who really
try are diminished into
something mortals only understand as unappreciated love;

while I live again in them.
And you.

It's sick, but it's love.
Friends wretch at it only because they're jealous.

I wouldn't believe it if I didn't live it but love does indeed conquer
all,
and fool all the rest, the rest of the time.

As much as I denied it, I was caught up in it
and cried at the beauty of what
I never thought I'd have.

ETERNAL VALENTINES

Be it Maui
> Kaanapali
> midday rendezvous
> topped with whipped cream

Be it Key West
> Islamorada exactly
> on the highway
> in the seat

Be it Paris
> City of Love
> open windows
> to the streets

Be it Vegas
> 20 year honeymoon
> overflowing jacuzzi
> top floor suite

Be it _____
> (you name it)
> this crazy life
> this wild love
> this   WEEE…

WORLD'S TO SHARE WITH YOU

The air that holds
your breath out in front of you,
that taunts and shows you how
close it really is to autumn,
is so different at night's
early morning,
from the busy air of day.

The night is crystal and sharp,
music slightly falling from
a clock radio
in a direct line to your hearing,
suspending it like the stars that
glitter in the falling
sky,
enveloping you in the sound
of nothing,
a fish
in his aquarium;
the sound of everything,
the sound of nothing.
So much more appealing than the
sound after a screen door closes.
(9/82)

I SNOW YOU

Why does the snow
remind me of you,
and those cold, bright,
cascading days in Kalamazoo?

Days that passed slowly
as we went to school.
Taking our time,
not rushing like tools

Watch as it falls
so straight and so perfect
Each flake a masterpiece,
never a defect

It knows where it's heading
it's path is straight down
But not finished yet
it piles the ground

I suppose that's its purpose
to make scenes change,
to bring beauty, build balance,
to make the familiar, strange.

So why does the snow
remind me of you?
Because what I see
Is hidden from view.

.

LIGHT THE DARK

I kiss your cheek
in the dark light.
You won't wake,
don't even stir.

You dream in endless
symbolicized scenes
While I watch
reality pass, redundantly
in front of me.

I shut your door and
Open mine to the
moon outside.
Who waits smiling slightly?

My car drives me
11 minutes to work.
One last look at
the starred sky;
One deep breath
To hold through the
fluorescent, windowless night.

Staring silent daydreams
of us in a better life.
I wonder who
You're seeing.
Tonight?

I OWE YOU

I owe it to you
The way I act cool
The times I play fool
The things I say, do

You've given me class
and dreams
and truths

You've given me Love
and faith
and You.

HOME

The way she lays her
head beneath my chin
The warmth and the
heartbeat of embrace

The way her flesh
caresses my skin

The scent.

The simple
beauty of her face.

The tingling excitement
of touch.
Always finds me,
home.

THE GIRL I SEE

Green Eyes,
eyes that see me
eye to eye.

The Exact,
the other half,
the side that asks why.

The eyes that dream
with stars as their map.
The eyes that mean
I am your man.

Plan with me
I'll hold your hand
We will stand
with our heads in the sky.

To fly
to be a pact.

Believe, Green Eyes.
(2/12/86)

MONOGAMY

I woke in silence
to start my day;
my lover lay curled and warm;
back bent in cotton comfort,
hand curled to chin,
presence emanating in slumber's embrace.
I thanked the Lord
for this love
of so many years
who bore my sons
who soaked my pains
who shared this bed
and so much more
with only me.

QUEEN OF HEARTS

There's the butterfly
the mother
the lover
the buns;
the candies
the cat
and the numbered ones

So what do I write
this time around
do I act serious
or should I clown

There's all these possibilities
yet all has been said
either in soliloquies
or together in bed

One thing rings, returns to me
every year, right here in print
the proof our love has changed,
as the gaze outlasts the glint

So this Valentines' Day
I'll keep it simple
I have enough to hear your breath whisper
To smell the perfume so strategically placed
there, there and (oh, my!) that space.
To feel your bare skin shaven smooth just for me
God how you always aim to please

JUST PRACTICING

From the Green Meadow's trees
to Macatawa's shores
to the ocean
to public pools
to avoid being bored
we made love.
We made it until we were sore!
Practice makes perfect.
We've just made one more.

VACANT PRESENCE

Can't stop thinking that
you're way across the
state
I drank myself to sleep
last night
Awoke far too often for a
comfortable rest
I couldn't hear the baby
or your breath
Now morning's here, far
from electric
The cats whine for
milk and breakfast
The silence is shattering.
Presence is vacant.

DAYMARE

Can't get the thoughts of you
out of my head
images of passion in
last nights bed
I see you so clearly
each curve, each side
holding these dearly
until I see you tonight.

I lick my lips wondering what
you're thinking now
if only I could get to you
some way, some how.

I remember it like a very lucid dream,
where the things that you touch
reach out and touch you back.
A walk on air experience
that's half awake, half asleep.
I felt a strange gravity that seemed to pull at us,
my fingers to your touch.
I felt (so cliché) electricity between us.
that karma that makes you and I
US.

MISS MS.

I haven't been seeing
much of you
and when I have
I didn't give you enough attention
It must be one of those
ME times again

I watch in awe of
your transformation
seeing what I've taken for granted

Your hair is shortened, gone, abrvd.
body deflated, flattened, minus contents;
You comfort our son with excruciating patience
Still
Again
I turn to run
without direction
and think of the times
we stand in the dark
naked.

He fills your needs
and I get to see
what Love looks like
from the outside.

DANCE

We've danced this dance
as many nights as
there are stars
and yet I still
count your ribs
on my fingers
through your shirt.
Your breath and your scent
rise in mixing my thoughts,
mince my words of silence
to yours in this dance
of desire, of passion,
of nights we'll remember
embraced nose to ear.

I PIECE

You did more good
for me than I could

You saw something
every time I tried
to destroy everything

Yes, you made me.
Yes, you unmade me.

tore me apart cruelly
with your perfect mouth

made me know damn well
I had a heart
because it hurt like hell

Those memories are dreams
the dreams are fragments
you, me…
Who are they?
Blame and lies
and pain and pride
that won't admit that
You were the best fucking thing to ever happen.

www.ingramcontent.com/pod-product-compliance
Lightning Source LLC
Chambersburg PA
CBHW030013040426
42337CB00012BA/765